Inside Special Operations

DELTA FORCE

Counterterrorism Unit of the U.S. Army

Betty Burnett, Ph.D.

the rosen publishing group's
rosen central

For Marshall

Published in 2003 by The Rosen Publishing Group, Inc.
29 East 21st Street, New York, NY 10010

First Edition

Library of Congress Cataloging-in-Publication Data

Burnett, Betty
Delta Force : counterterrorism unit of the U.S. Army/Betty Burnett.
p. cm—(Inside special operations)
Includes bibliographical references and index.
Summary: This book presents a look at Delta Force, a special operations unit of the U.S. Army, including information on its beginnings, its assignments, and its successful missions.
ISBN 0-8239-3807-7
1. United States Army. Delta Force—History—Juvenile literature
2. Special forces (Military science)—United States—History—Juvenile literature [1. United States. Army. Delta Force 2. Special forces (Military science)]
I. Title II. Series
356'.1673'0973—dc21

2002113970

Manufactured in the United States of America

Contents

U.S. Army Special Forces soldiers practice HALO parachute jumps from an air force C-130 aircraft. These jumps give Delta Force troopers a better chance of entering enemy territory without being seen or captured.

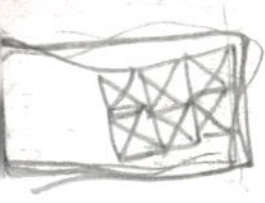

Introduction

Somewhere in an unnamed country, parachutes drop from a plane onto rock-studded mountains. It is after midnight, very dark and very cold. There is no sound but the clunk as each parachutist hits the ground.

Each man has a specific assignment. No one wastes time figuring out what to do next. Their job is to rescue Americans who are being held hostage at gunpoint. They have to make sure these Americans get home safely.

They've practiced their assignment dozens of times and have memorized everything about it—the timeline, the route they will take, the building they will enter, and where they will find the hostages. They have thought of all the things that could go wrong with the operation and have made plans about what to do in case there is a glitch.

They move silently toward their destination, dressed in black with face shields. Their night vision goggles allow them to see in the darkness. They carry no identification, but they do carry high-tech communication devices. Not only are they electronically connected to each other through the global positioning system (GPS), they are in touch with their headquarters and can monitor electronic communications coming from the hostage hideout.

This small group of men is part of a special operations (special ops) unit of the U.S. Army, highly trained and ready for anything. The men are armed with powerful weapons and will not hesitate to use them. They prefer not to take prisoners.

They are Delta Force.

1. Delta Force's Beginnings

When the Vietnam War ended in 1973, Americans thought it would be the beginning of world peace. Instead, a new, more frightening form of warfare emerged: terrorism. Terrorists are bullies on a large scale. They try to control people with fear, just the way any bully does. They threaten, hurt, and kill civilians. Sometimes they take ordinary people as hostages to force governments to give them what they want.

In the early days of terrorism, governments didn't know how to react to this threat. There was no visible enemy as there had been in earlier wars. How could anyone fight an enemy they couldn't see? No one knew when, where, or how terrorists would strike. They often hit where and when people least expected because terrorism relies on surprise and random attack.

Counterterrorism forces—people who want to stop terrorism—knew they had to gather all the information they could find on terrorist groups and tactics so they could plan how to fight back. Terrorist tactics became well known in the 1970s: kidnapping people, taking hostages, assassinating political leaders, detonating car bombs, and hijacking airplanes. Over the past thirty years, terrorist attacks have gotten more sophisticated and more deadly.

In 1997, according to *U.S. News & World Report*, 304 terrorist attacks occurred around the globe, or almost one a day in spite of increased security everywhere. Most of these attacks received little attention in the United States because they did not involve Americans. Terrorism causes feelings of panic and helplessness. In many areas of the world, especially in the Middle East, people never feel safe.

Terrorists first got attention by hijacking airplanes. Between 1970 and 1980, according to the magazine *Aviation Security and Aviation Safety*, 384 airplanes were hijacked around the world, putting their passengers and crews at serious risk. In 1970 alone, seventy-seven planes were taken over by terrorists, more than one a week. The problem in the

The Special Force Operational Detachment-Delta, or Delta Force, was formed in response to the increase in airplane hijackings and other terrorist acts in the 1970s.

United States was bigger than either the airlines or the Federal Bureau of Investigation (FBI) could handle.

One American, Colonel Charles Beckwith, a veteran of the Green Beret Project Delta unit in Vietnam, watched the increase in hijackings with alarm. He wanted the army to do something about it. His training with the British Special Air Service (SAS) convinced him that the U.S. Army needed a similar unit. Throughout the early 1970s, he proposed that the army build a top-secret, fast-moving squad of

"Chargin' Charlie" Beckwith 1929–1994

Charles Beckwith was born near Atlanta, Georgia, in 1929. He grew up to be a 6´3˝ all-star football player who served in the ROTC in high school and at the University of Georgia. He chose the regular U.S. Army as a career, then left it to become a Green Beret in Vietnam. There he earned a reputation as a tough, daring and decisive soldier. Because he was always willing to take a risk and liked to move fast, he was given the nickname "Chargin' Charlie." As an officer, his men liked and respected him. In turn, he had a soft heart for their welfare. He searched for those who were missing and openly cried when he lost a man.

counterterrorists. In 1974, army officials told him to go ahead and write up a plan and they'd study it.

In 1976, the plan was accepted. The Special Force Operational Detachment-Delta (SFOD-D) unit was officially organized in 1980. Its original purpose was to free hostages, whether in captivity on the ground or in a hijacked aircraft. The force gradually formed into a counterterrorist unit with support personnel, and aviation, medical, and communication divisions. Perhaps other, classified divisions have also been formed.

Special Ops vs. Regular Forces

Special ops are different from regular forces in several ways. The regular armed forces must work within a rigid set of rules, and there are strict procedures they must follow. They don't have the latitude that special ops have, and could be court-martialed for some of the things the special ops do. Their training is usually not top secret or classified. It also may have very little to do with combat and more to do with administration and technology.

Regular troops are divided up into large units. They move slowly because of their large numbers and because they must carry supplies and equipment. Special ops forces are streamlined and fast moving. They pay little attention to rank or privilege. They often work outside the rules and ignore "by-the-book" procedures. They do what works—they may wear disguises, and they may deny knowledge of their mission. When they land in a foreign country, they may work with the existing military or police officials or they may ignore them. Instead of waiting for orders from a commander about what to do, special ops must be able to make quick decisions on their own, knowing that those decisions may be unpopular back home. The media, politicians, and even the regular military have criticized Delta Force for its unorthodox methods.

The exact number of special ops members in all the U.S. armed forces is not known. A *Fortune* magazine article recently estimated their numbers at 30,000, compared to 1.5 million regular troops. This number includes the Green Berets, Navy SEALs, Army Rangers, and secret air force units, as well as Delta Force. It is likely that there are fewer than 5,000 Delta Force members today.

Old-Style Ground War vs. New-Style Combat

The Vietnam War may turn out to be the last long-term conventional ground war fought by the United States. Both technology and politics have changed since then. Now, small cultural groups fight each other within national borders,

U.S. Special Forces operatives patrol the outskirts of Kandahar Airport in Afghanistan after the terrorist attacks on September 11, 2001. It is likely that Delta Force has led the search for Al Qaeda leader Osama bin Laden.

instead of nations fighting nations. The enemy may be a slippery organization of fanatical groups, like the terrorist network Al Qaeda, with shifting headquarters and a "hit-and-run" style of attack.

These groups are too small to build a large army and don't have enough money for expensive weapons or uniforms. Members are willing to die for their cause and are unwilling to negotiate a truce. Suicide bombers blow themselves up along with other people who happen to be in the wrong place at the wrong time.

Today, military units everywhere must respond quickly to terrorist attacks. They must try to anticipate what sort of attack could happen next and where. They don't have time to plan battles with thousands of soldiers.

Intelligence has become much more important than massed force. A Delta Force slogan claims, "Your mind is your best weapon." Brainpower can stop terrorism as fast as firepower. The job is to outthink the enemy, as well as to outshoot him. Smart weapons and smart soldiers are two of America's best counterterrorism resources.

Delta Force troops on horseback in northern Afghanistan. A large part of their mission there is to gather information that will help the United States in its fight against the Al Qaeda terrorist network.

Instant communication is a vital part of today's combat. Delta Force uses palm-sized computers, cell phones, and radios to link with each other and to receive information. They learn the language of their enemies so they can intercept messages from them and find out their plans. They need to know world geography, foreign languages, different types of cultures, and world history. All this knowledge is part of their arsenal.

All special ops units are trained in detective work. They look and listen for clues about possible terrorist strikes, and they hunt down and capture terrorists and other international criminals who imprison, torture, and murder people to become powerful.

Delta Force, along with other special ops, also provides security at major international events, such as the Olympic Games, where terrorists might attack. They keep the area safe for both participants and spectators by never letting their guard down.

Terrorism is global. Terrorists may strike anywhere on Earth. Delta Force and other special ops troops have responded to emergencies in South America, Central America, the Persian Gulf, southern Europe, and the Middle East. We can assume—even though the government may not verify it—that Delta Force is at work in most of the "hot spots" on the globe, wherever civilians are in danger.

2. Rescue

Delta Force was created to rescue hostages. For a rescue operation to be successful, everything must work together smoothly. There is no advance warning of a hostage capture. The rescue unit must be able to go anywhere in the world at a moment's notice and be ready for any condition—jungle heat or Arctic cold. They must be able to communicate in any language used anywhere on the globe. They must choose the best gear to bring, and they must take the most appropriate weapons from their arsenal. There is no time for indecision.

To plan a rescue mission, hundreds of questions must be answered quickly. The answers may come from

Delta Force operatives are often up against terrorists who seek publicity for their cause. Here, hooded hijackers show their potential for danger at a press conference.

intelligence agents in the field or they may come from the terrorists themselves. Sometimes terrorists seek publicity and want their hostages photographed, videotaped, and interviewed. The Red Cross, Red Crescent, or another humanitarian organization may be allowed to talk to the hostages and bring back important information: Where are the hostages being held? How many are there? What are their ages, sizes, and health? Does someone need medication? Has anyone been injured? How many nationalities are involved? If there are citizens of other countries involved, the U.S. government will have to work with those governments.

Once they know everything they can about the hostages, Delta Force members (along with other special ops units) have to figure out how to reach them. Every detail is important. Is the building where they are held made of brick, wood, stone, or adobe? Are the hostages held in prison cells or ordinary rooms? Have they been divided up or are they all together? Where are the light switches? What kind of furniture is in the rooms? Are the windows boarded up or glass? How many doors are there and what kind of locks are on them? What's the best entrance and exit? Maybe they'll have to blow a hole in the wall. Delta ops like to work at night. Will that make things easier or more difficult? Will weather be a factor? Intense heat or cold, high winds, a snowstorm, a sandstorm, or an electrical storm would add challenges. Most important, once they get in to where the hostages are being held, how will they get safely out with them? Where will they take them? And how much time will they have?

All these questions must be answered before Delta Force can make a rescue plan. After a plan is made, the next step is to rehearse it as many times as they can. Only then can they go forward.

Operation Eagle Claw

Delta Force's first assignment was to rescue hostages held at the U.S. Embassy in Tehran, Iran. In January 1979, an uprising in Iran forced the shah (king) into exile. After a period of upheaval, the shah eventually came to the United States and the Ayatollah Ruholla Khomeini took over the leadership in Iran. Khomeini's followers demanded that the shah be returned to Iran for a trial. The U.S. government refused to send him. In protest, three thousand Iranians invaded the U.S. Embassy in Tehran, taking sixty-six Americans hostage. Thirteen hostages were soon freed for humanitarian reasons, but the remaining fifty-three were held for fourteen months.

The American hostages were held captive for 444 days in Iran. Despite several attempts, such as putting economic pressure on Iran and ordering military rescue missions, President Jimmy Carter failed to bring the hostages home. They were finally released on January 20, 1981.

Colonel Charlie Beckwith saw this situation as perfect for launching Delta Force. When negotiations with Khomeini didn't work to release the hostages, President Jimmy Carter agreed to a military rescue. Beckwith and other military leaders spent months planning the rescue operation, code-named Eagle Claw.

The city of Tehran is isolated, surrounded by 700 miles of desert and rugged mountains. To begin with, Delta Force had to figure out how to get into the city. Helicopters seemed the best option. They could hover over the embassy and men could "fast rope" down from them without needing to parachute.

Navy Sea Stallion helicopters were chosen because they could carry a lot of weight. But they could not fly from an aircraft carrier in the Persian Gulf to Tehran without refueling. Planners decided to use air force C-130 Hercules transport planes rigged with extra fuel tanks to refuel the helicopters somewhere on their way to Tehran.

Next they had to find a spot in the Iranian desert where the helicopters could land for refueling. The ground where they landed would have to support the weight of the heavy air transports—not easy to find in the deep sands of the desert. Intelligence teams located a site about 200 miles southeast of Tehran. This rendezvous point, where helicopters, tankers, and Delta Force would meet, was code-named Desert One.

Planners turned their attention to the buildings where the hostages were being held. The layout of the U.S. Embassy compound was well known, but no one knew exactly where the hostages were. Were they all together in one area or spread out among the six buildings? Beckwith decided that Delta would have to search all six buildings. He assigned enough men and helicopters to the mission to allow the six buildings to be searched at the same time. Extra helicopters would be needed to bring out the fifty-three hostages. Eight helicopters—certainly no fewer than six—would be needed for so many people.

In the early months of 1980, helicopter crews of various U.S. special ops units practiced the mission around Yuma, Arizona, while others rehearsed in Florida and Guam. The newly organized Delta Force trained in the woods of North Carolina. A mock-up of the embassy compound was built for practice. A staff in Washington directed the entire operation. Information bounced between the sites reporting on what they were doing, but the crews did not get a chance to work together before the operation.

The Disaster at Desert One

By mid-March 1980, after five months of planning and rehearsals, it seemed as if everything was in place. The plan was for 132 Delta ops, Army Rangers, and various support personnel to fly to Desert One in the middle of the night. Army transports would bring the necessary fuel for the helicopters. Eight Navy Sea Stallions, code-named Bluebirds, would fly 600 miles to meet them there.

As soon as the helicopters refueled, they would fly the troopers to a spot fifty miles southeast of Tehran. After hiding out during the day, Delta Force ops and Army Rangers would invade the embassy in Tehran the next night and free the hostages. The helicopters would be there to pick everyone up. During the operation, three air force gunships would fly overhead to protect the rescue forces from counterattack. Once aboard the helicopters, the hostages and rescue force would fly to an abandoned air base southwest of Tehran that was protected by Army Rangers.

It sounded good on paper. On April 11, 1980, President Carter gave the go-ahead for the mission, saying it was time to bring the hostages home. The date for Eagle Claw was set for April 24. On that day, forty-four aircraft were at their appointed stations as planned. The weather report was good: clear skies and maximum visibility. A message was relayed from headquarters: "Execute mission as planned."

Shortly after the helicopters lifted off, a warning light came on in the cockpit of Bluebird 6. The craft had to land at once to avoid crashing. Then an unexpected sandstorm came up. Bluebird 5 reported nearly zero visibility and turned back. The other six choppers were slowed by the storm but kept going. They landed in deep sand at Desert One. The mushy ground was something they hadn't planned on. A critical system in Bluebird 2 abruptly failed. Now three helicopters were down and only five were usable. Five was not enough. Beckwith felt the mission could not continue. He ordered everyone back to the base.

As one of the helicopters lifted off, full of men, it slid sideways, slicing into a transport plane loaded with fuel.

Operation Eagle Claw proved to be a disaster. The wreckage shown above is of the doomed C-130 cargo aircraft that collided with a helicopter.

Both aircraft ignited in a tremendous explosion. Fire, pieces of hot steel, and burning fuel rained down on the troops. Eight men were killed. Many more were badly injured.

The disaster was a tremendous setback for Delta Force and an embarrassment for the Carter administration. The media blamed "poor planning" because the military hadn't expected that so many things would go wrong.

All further negotiations to release the hostages were called off. After holding them for nine more months, Khomeini finally released them in January 1981, just as Ronald Reagan was taking the oath of office to become president of the United States.

Timeline

1977–1979—Delta Force formed

1979—Present at the Pan American Games in Puerto Rico as part of an antiterrorist team

1980—Operation Eagle Claw at Desert One

1981—Joined the search for an American general kidnapped by terrorists in Italy

1982—Sent to Honduras as security guards in Operation Queens Hunter

1983—Operation Urgent Fury in Grenada

1984—Operation Manta in Libya and Chad

1985—Deployed to Algeria after a TWA airliner was hijacked

1986—Part of the security team at the Statue of Liberty Centennial

1987—Sent to Greece in response to reports that Vietnamese communist agents were going to kidnap an American army officer

1989—Operation Just Cause in Panama

1991—Deployed to the Persian Gulf as bodyguards for U.S. officers and to destroy Scud missiles

1992—Sent to Waco, Texas, as part of an assault on the Branch Davidian compound

1993—Joined Task Force Ranger in Mogadishu, Somalia, during UN operations

1994—Operation Uphold Democracy in Haiti

1995—Hunt for war criminals in Bosnia

1997—Sent to Lima, Peru, following the takeover of the Japanese ambassador's residence

1998—Operation Allied Force in Kosovo

2001—Joined the search for Osama bin Laden in Afghanistan

3. A Professional Unit

Congress investigated the disaster at Desert One right away. They found that the biggest problem was disorganization. The U.S. Army, Navy, Marines, and Air Force were each involved, but separately, not together.

Colonel Beckwith and other military leaders testified that special ops from all branches of the military needed to be put together in one special operations force (SOF) with its own rules and chain of command. Congress agreed and changes were made. This made planning and carrying out missions much easier.

Throughout the 1980s, special ops units received several important assignments. Sometimes they worked together—Navy SEALs and Delta Force, for instance, or Army Rangers and air force units. They learned to communicate with each other quickly and to share information. Their intelligence units worked harder, knowing that lives depended on what they could find out.

Two of Delta Force's rescue missions made the news in the 1980s. Both were successful, but neither was perfect.

Operation Urgent Fury

In the early 1980s, about 1,000 Americans were living on the tiny island of Grenada in the Caribbean Sea, just north of Venezuela. Many of them were students attending St. George Medical School in the capital city of St. George. Intelligence reports indicated that Grenada was strongly influenced by Cuban communism, which at that time seemed to threaten the United States. Agents reported great numbers of Soviet weapons arriving on the island. In the fall of 1983, a group called the People's Revolutionary Army took over the government of Grenada by force and killed its leaders. Violence broke out all over the island. It looked as if Americans were in danger.

In mid-October, the new Grenadan government announced that no American citizens would be allowed to leave the island. That meant that they were being held prisoner there,

U.S. military helicopters are prepared for the invasion of Grenada. Delta Force operatives were ordered to rescue political prisoners, but were only partially successful in their attempts.

even though they still lived in their apartments and were allowed to attend school as usual.

After hearing intelligence reports, President Ronald Reagan ordered U.S. military units to Grenada to bring home all of the Americans. It was a sudden decision and a surprise operation—most of the soldiers didn't know where they were going until they were a few miles away, and none of the Americans on the island were alerted. Suddenly, U.S. Navy ships and air force fighter planes, gunships, and helicopters converged on the island. Thousands of special ops and regular military parachuted down, while Navy SEALs arrived by boat. Each unit had a different assignment.

Delta Force had two primary objectives—to clear out Fort Rupert and Richmond Hill Prison. Fort Rupert housed the Revolutionary Council, the leaders of the new government. Delta troopers arrived there by helicopter, quickly rounded up their prisoners, and sent them off to Guam for questioning.

Richmond Hill Prison was not so easy. Hundreds of Grenada's citizens were being held there without charges against them. They were political prisoners, not criminals. Delta ops and Army Rangers were ordered to rescue them. As the troopers came into the area by helicopter, they found it heavily defended, with large guns surrounding the prison. They hadn't counted on that because intelligence reports had not mentioned such firepower. Anti-aircraft fire from Grenadan forces shot down one helicopter. The officers knew that many of their men would be shot if they fast-roped down from the helicopters. They decided to retreat. A little later they tried a second assault, but it wasn't successful either. Over the next few days, U.S. troops fanned out over the island, evacuating Americans and closing down Grenadan military operations.

Operation Acid Gambit

American Kurt Muse worked in his family's business in Panama during the 1980s, selling printing and graphic arts equipment throughout Central America. He became concerned as he watched General Manuel Noriega become powerful through military force. Panama is a democracy, with a constitution similar to that of the United States. Muse could see that Noriega was trying to end democracy and turn the country into a dictatorship by frightening off everyone who opposed him through imprisonment, torture, and murder.

In 1989, Muse decided to build a secret radio station to broadcast anti-Noriega messages. His first broadcast came during Noriega's official state address to the Panamanian people. Instead of hearing Noriega, the radio audience heard a two-minute message from "the free democratic people of Panama."

Noriega was furious and sent his soldiers to arrest those involved in the pirate radio station, but they couldn't find them. For the next two months, the broadcasts continued. Noriega thought that Muse was one of the "pirates." Posters with Muse's photograph went up in Panama City. An army official at the airport recognized Muse as he got off a plane from Florida and had him arrested.

After three days of questioning, Muse was sent to the Carcel Modelo, an old prison crowded with four times as many prisoners as it was built to hold. Every day Muse heard the screams of men being tortured. He was rarely let out of his cell and was given so little to eat that he lost fifty pounds. A soldier was assigned to guard his cell with standing orders to kill him if the United States took any action against Panama. That turned him into a hostage.

In the United States, President George Bush told military commanders to rescue Muse. The job was given to Delta Force, along with the 160th Special Operations Aviation Regiment (SOAR). They would be supported by a naval gunship stationed in the Bay of Panama alongside Panama City within range of the prison.

Planning for Operation Acid Gambit began. In a remote area of Florida, a full-scale, three-story mock-up of the prison was built. Small helicopters ("Little Birds") practiced landing on the roof of the building. Delta Force commandos rehearsed the rescue—they would use explosives to open the door to the roof, then fight their way down to Muse's cell on the second floor, capture him, return to the helicopters on the roof, and take off, all in a couple of minutes.

Complicating the plan was the fact that the headquarters (commandancia) of the Panama Defense Force was right across the street from the prison. U.S. undercover special ops were already in Panama City gathering information on the strength and location of other military units.

On December 20, 1989, at 12:45 AM, Operation Acid Gambit began. It was scheduled to take less than five minutes. U.S. planes fired rockets into the commandancia compound, keeping Noriega's soldiers busy there. Two large helicopters circled the compound, firing constantly. Sharpshooting sniper teams were posted on buildings near the prison. Within moments they killed several guards. Then the sharpshooters aimed at the prison generator and fired. The interior of the prison went black as it lost electricity.

Almost immediately, the four Little Bird helicopters, each with four commandos on board, touched down on the roof of the prison. As practiced, they blasted open the rooftop door and ran down the steps to the second floor, firing as they went. In his cell, Muse heard an American voice holler, "Take cover!" He ducked and the cell door exploded open. A Delta op, in black protective gear, rushed in and handed Muse a helmet and flak vest. The two men raced back upstairs.

On the roof, the commandos got back in the helicopters and took off. The pilot in Muse's chopper had to pull straight up to avoid power lines. The maneuver didn't work. The chopper quickly lost altitude and flew only a few feet off the ground through the narrow streets of Panama City. Another attempt to take off succeeded, but then gunfire brought the helicopter down. The men took cover in a nearby building. After about fifteen minutes, using an infrared strobe light, they were able to signal aircraft flying overhead, which alerted a nearby U.S. Army patrol in an armed personnel carrier. These soldiers were able to rescue everyone.

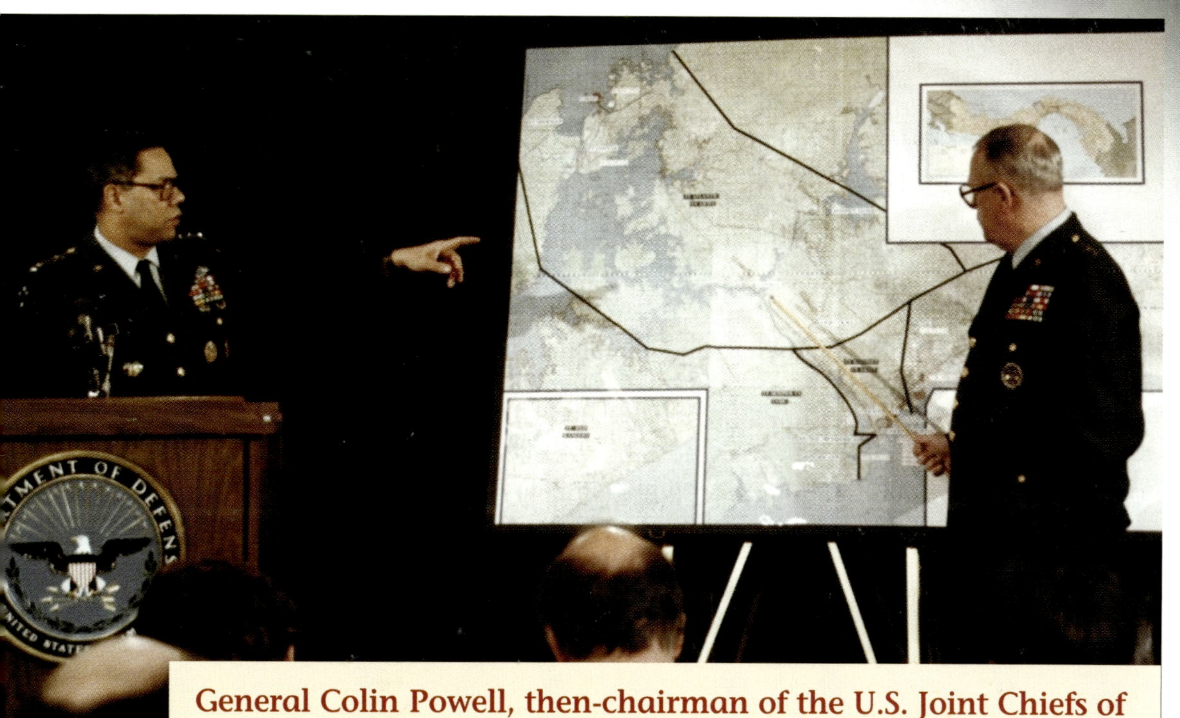

General Colin Powell, then-chairman of the U.S. Joint Chiefs of Staff, briefs the press about Operation Acid Gambit. After seven hours of the military operation, at least nine American soldiers had been killed and Manuel Noriega was still at large.

Hijacking

Increased airport security cut down on the number of hijacked U.S. airplanes in the 1980s, although they still occurred. SOF units were frequently sent to rescue hostages after a hijacking, but the situation was always resolved before they could do anything. The closest Delta Force came to rescuing hijacked passengers was not on an airplane, but on a ship.

In October 1985, some 400 passengers were enjoying the sun and sparkling water on the Italian cruise ship the *Achille*

Lauro. Suddenly, four heavily armed members of the Palestinian Liberation Organization (PLO) forced their way on board and demanded that fifty Palestinian prisoners being held in Israel be freed.

To show they were serious, terrorists killed an elderly, disabled American, Leon Klinghoffer, and threw his body overboard, along with his wheelchair. The world was appalled by this cowardly act. After two days, with Delta Force and a Navy SEAL team on their way, the hijackers surrendered to the Egyptian government, and the ship was free to go to port.

4. Assignment: Danger

One of the tough jobs assigned to Delta Force is capturing international criminals who have broken either U.S. law or United Nations (UN) law. Terrorism is against international law, of course, but so are other crimes, such as mass murder, smuggling drugs or weapons, and being involved in the human slave trade. Capturing international criminals alive is very difficult and often impossible. Special ops forces have to use all their skills to stop these criminals from doing more harm in the world.

In addition to hunting for criminals, Delta Force troopers work behind enemy lines. This highly secret work is also their most dangerous. Many troopers have been killed or injured in combat. Their battles often start with a nighttime raid and end with hand-to-hand fighting. They have become experts in urban warfare.

Delta Force troopers were present in Beirut, Lebanon, in the 1980s. In 1984, they took part in Operation Manta in Africa, which began in Chad and reached into Libya. In the late 1980s, they were present in civil wars fought in Central America. More is known about their efforts in the Gulf War of 1990–1991.

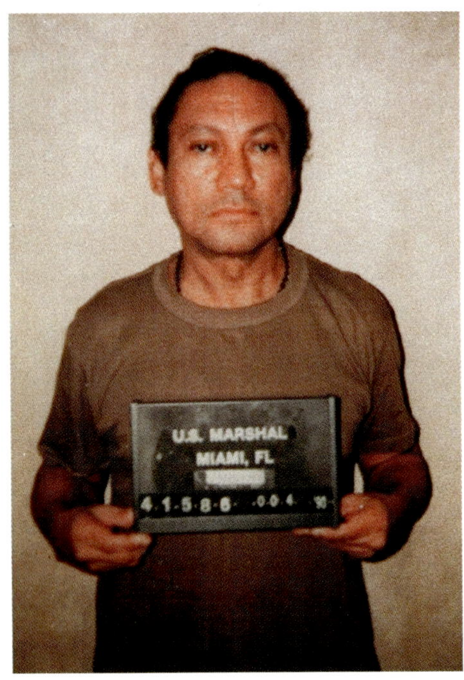

A great foe of democracy, General Manuel Noriega of Panama was finally seized, convicted, and sentenced to forty years in prison.

Drug-Busting

The United States considers drug trafficking a serious crime. Much of the illegal drug trade in this country—especially in cocaine and heroin—comes from South and Central America. In some countries, so-called drug lords stake out their territory and kill anyone who tries to interfere with their operation. They not only break laws, they care nothing for the people of their country.

In the late 1980s, General Manuel Noriega was the head of the Panama Defense Forces. U.S. officials thought he was also directing a criminal ring and smuggling illegal drugs into the United States. The U.S. government wanted to stop the trade. Delta Force was probably involved in his capture—called Operation Just Cause—although their role is not clear.

Another well-known drug lord was Pablo Escobar. He ran a very successful illegal drug operation in Colombia. Because they considered him responsible for smuggling millions of dollars worth of illegal drugs into the United States, the Drug Enforcement Agency (DEA) went after him. Delta Force and Navy SEALs joined them. Delta Force ops located Escobar at his estate and were prepared to storm the place, but they didn't have the support of Colombian officials. Later, Colombian police and U.S. forces hunted down Escobar and killed him.

Black Hawk Down

The Delta Force operation in the African country of Somalia lasted less than twenty-four hours, but it is well known through the book *Black Hawk Down* by Mark Bowden and the movie made from the book. The Somali warlord, General

Mohamed Farrah Aidid, and his henchmen had come to power through murder, torture, and theft. The United Nations intervened because civilians were at risk. They sent in an international peacekeeping force.

For their part in the peacekeeping operation, the United States sent in a large joint task force with Delta ops, SEALs, Army Rangers, and Night Stalkers to clear the area of these terrorists. On October 3, 1993, the assault began in central Mogadishu, the capital city of Somalia. As an Army Ranger was fast-roping from the helicopter, he fell seventy feet (about twenty-one meters) to the street and was critically injured. The others tried to

Black Hawk helicopters are used for air assault, air cavalry, and medical evacuation missions. Black Hawks have been used in missions in Somalia, Grenada, Panama, the Persian Gulf War, Haiti, and Bosnia. They cost about $6 million each and are designed to resist small arms fire and some projectiles.

rescue their man and were immediately surrounded by the Somalia militia. A vicious firefight ensued.

Delta ops went ahead with their mission and captured twenty of Aidid's top lieutenants. A support convoy of Humvees and trucks approached to take the U.S. forces back to base. As they reached the commandos, gunfire erupted from all sides. At the same time, a Night Stalker's Black Hawk helicopter was struck by a missile, causing it to crash. The Humvee convoy was rerouted to help the pilot but got lost. For five hours the soldiers fought for their lives in what was described as "the largest firefight since Vietnam." The unit was finally rescued by Pakistani and Malaysian peacekeeping troops. Eighteen Rangers and Delta troopers were killed and more than seventy were wounded before they got back to base.

Project Green Light

Bosnia-Herzegovina in southern Europe was the center of conflict during the mid-1990s. Religious and ethnic groups with a long-standing hatred for each other tore their nation apart. Each side accused the other of atrocities. Even before the war ended, a UN tribunal indicted military leaders to try them for war crimes, especially for the torture and killing of civilians. In one terrible incident, 8,000 unarmed Muslim men and boys were massacred at Srebrenica.

As soon as the Dayton Peace Accord was signed in 1995, the military officers responsible for the massacre went into hiding. International special ops forces, including more than a hundred members of Delta Force, were dispatched to capture five of the "persons indicted for war crimes," or PIFWCs (pronounced pif-wix). Using undercover surveillance, special ops located many of the war criminals, but they were not able to track down all of them. Delta Force is probably still involved in the hunt for PIFWCs, but information about their operation is classified.

Operation Desert Storm

In 1980, Iraq invaded Iran and began a war that lasted until 1988. Saddam Hussein, Iraq's leader, wanted his country to become the most powerful one in the Persian Gulf. He didn't have the manpower to attack the large countries, such as Egypt, Syria, and Saudi Arabia, directly. Instead, his strategy was to build a large arsenal of long-range ballistic missiles. Some of these missiles were launched from fixed sites; others were on mobile launchers. The most famous were the Scud missiles. Because the Scud could be fired into cities from so far away, it was a weapon of terror. Counterterrorists began to get ready to act.

In August 1990, Iraqi troops invaded the small neighboring country of Kuwait, planning to take over its oil reserves.

Military troops examine a Gulf War Scud missile that was shot down in the desert of Saudi Arabia. The Delta Force teamed up with the British SAS to destroy Scud launching sites.

The United Nations and the United States immediately protested and prepared for combat. In January 1991, without warning, Iraq sent a barrage of Scud missiles to Israel, destroying apartment houses and killing civilians. UN forces decided they had to destroy the Scuds to prevent an all-out war in the Middle East.

Two special operations groups were given the job of locating and destroying Scud launch sites—the British SAS and the U.S. Delta Force. Delta Force was assigned to "Scud Boulevard," near Al Aim, Iraq. They infiltrated the country by helicopter and traveled on the ground in fast attack vehicles (FAVs) by night, hiding out during the day. Each FAV carried two or three fully-equipped soldiers; food; water; weapons, such as antitank missiles, grenade launchers, and machine guns; ammunition; and extra fuel. The soldiers carried laser target designators to locate the Scuds and used long-range .50-caliber sniper rifles to disable and destroy them. This was one of Delta Force's most successful missions.

Operation Allied Force

Kosovo is a southern province of Yugoslavia, a country in southern Europe. Kosovo borders Albania, and many people of Albanian heritage (the so-called ethnic Albanians) live in Kosovo. The government is run by Serbians, however, and the president, Slobodan Milosevic, encouraged and even ordered harsh measures against the ethnic Albanians. In response, the Albanians formed the Kosovo Liberation Army (KLA) and called for full independence from Serbian rule.

In 1997, the KLA began targeting and killing Serbian policemen and other officials in Kosovo and eventually gained control over part of the area. President Milosevic sent Serbian troops into Kosovo to crush the KLA in February 1998. Many civilians were killed in the violence that followed, and as many as 200,000 people lost their homes. NATO decided to send in troops, including Delta Force, to protect the civilians from crimes against humanity.

Although their assignment in Operation Allied Force was secret, it is thought that Delta soldiers gathered information about Serbian plans and, as undercover ops, followed Serbian troops. In the spring of 1999, after NATO planes bombed the area, Milosevic agreed to talk about peace. By then, over half a million Kosovars had become refugees and their country had been almost destroyed. Today, people are trying to rebuild their homes and towns, but there is still unrest and the threat of more violence. It is likely that Delta Force is still in Kosovo, watching and waiting.

Afghanistan

Although not much is known yet about the role of Delta Force in the search for Osama bin Laden and the members of Al Qaeda in Afghanistan at the time of this printing, authorities have acknowledged that Delta Force is there, along with other special ops units. Probably they are doing what they do best—working undercover and smoking out the enemy.

5. High-Tech Warfare

Combat is high-tech today, and tomorrow's warriors will have capabilities and equipment only imagined now. *Popular Science* describes this "future soldier" as a grownup Power Ranger whose uniform will change colors to fade into the environment, like a chameleon. The new lightweight, waterproof uniform will have temperature controls that switch from cool to warm in seconds. It will be flame resistant and will protect the wearer against chemical and biological weapons. Sensors will monitor vital signs, so medics can instantly tell the condition of a wounded soldier.

A zoom camera in the soldier's helmet will allow him a close-up look at everything around him. His rifle will have a thermal site, one that automatically aims at warm bodies, and he'll carry more software in his backpack than hardware.

Because today's soldiers are more technology-minded than those in the past, they play a larger part in the development of high-tech weapons and equipment.

Today, special ops forces are testing new equipment that will make them more efficient and safe. Much of this equipment is navigational—it tells soldiers where they are and where they are going, giving routes and mileages. They already use palm and "backtop" computers. Backtops—called land warriors—are small enough to be carried in a backpack. Each one has a GPS receiver, a miniature camera, a laser rangefinder, video (day) and thermal (night) weapons sights, and a radio.

The GPS system produces a digitized map that instantly tells the soldier where he is. The rangefinder calculates the exact distance to a target and locates it on the map. It can relay this information to everyone in the squad or to remote-controlled, unmanned flying drones that will bomb the target.

The ground laser target designator is a portable laser that guides a bomb or missile to its target. These small missiles will be programmed to follow their targets and will be launched from a soldier's arm, like an arrow from a bow.

Today's small computers can send and receive information in code, in case a hacker taps in. In some cases, they can translate information intercepted from the enemy into English. They connect to radios and to satellite phones that can reach all around the globe.

Night vision goggles (NVGs) are indispensable equipment for catching an enemy unaware. NVGs work using infrared or thermal imaging technology.

Most strikes or rescue operations take place at night. Night vision goggles (NVGs) are worn on a helmet or hand shield. Helicopter pilots wear them, too. The goggles amplify light from the moon and stars millions of times. They don't yet work during dust storms, rain, or fog.

Special ops soldiers today wear ALICE packs—all-purpose lightweight individual carrying equipment backpacks. ALICE packs are designed to distribute the weight of the pack evenly over the upper back to eliminate muscle strain. Soldiers typically carry 100 pounds of personal gear, more than half their body weight. This extra weight slows them down. Lighter equipment will allow soldiers to run faster and dodge bullets better.

Vehicles

Delta Force works with the Special Operation Aviation Regiment (SOAR), called Night Stalkers. Their black helicopters are specially equipped so they can fly very low to the ground. They also can fly at night and in bad weather without bright lights. They are armored, so they can stand up to anti-aircraft guns, and are equipped with flares that act like fireworks to confuse heat-seeking missiles coming from the enemy.

Some helicopters are able to land and take off from the decks of navy ships so they don't need a heliport. It is rumored that silent helicopters are being developed. These would allow a Delta Force operation to go undetected until the very last minute.

Delta Force ops usually fast-rope down from a helicopter. Sometimes they must parachute from a plane. The HAHO (High Altitude-High Opening) parachute was made especially for them. It allows jumpers to keep their hands down at their sides during their descent, rather than up in the air, holding on to the rigging as is usual. Even before they land they are able to fire a weapon if necessary.

Although Special Forces are often transported by air or sea so that they can operate in secrecy, sometimes land vehicles are more effective.

Predator drones are not only used as weapons. Sometimes they fly over a target, taking infrared or video images of the ground below. This gives the troops important information about the strength of the enemy before they attack.

Land vehicles for desert terrain or mountains have been designed for special ops units. They are equipped with GPS systems and are heavily armed. Fast attack vehicles—a cross between a jeep and a dune buggy—were successfully used in the Gulf War.

Weapons

The arsenal available to special ops today is enormous. Many weapons are specially made for them and are top secret. Delta Force is armed with guns, rockets, grenades, and knives. They carry several types of guns, usually a pistol, combat rifle, sniper rifle, and submachine gun. They are masters of the martial arts and can use their bodies, as well as their hardware, as weapons.

Warfare in the years ahead will likely continue to be urban warfare—street fighting in cities. Delta Force can expect rooftop snipers, alleyway ambushes, and booby-trapped buildings in their rescue operations. They must think fast and move fast. They must decide when to fire and when not to, always remembering their mission to keep civilians safe.

6. What It Takes to Join Delta Force

For every spot in Delta Force, as many as 100 people may apply. Only the toughest, smartest, and healthiest soldiers get accepted into the training program. Once they are in, they must work hard to stay in. The training program is so tough that many applicants drop out.

Most Delta Force ops come from the regular army or Army Rangers. They have already gone through basic training and even advanced training. Sometimes, someone with a special skill is asked to join.

The general requirements for Delta Force are exceptional physical fitness, mental toughness, self-confidence, and loyalty to the group. These requirements are tested over and over during training.

SFQC Training

General training for all army special ops units takes place at Fort Bragg, North Carolina. The Special Forces Qualification Course (SFQC) usually lasts about thirty days. The army recommends that anyone who starts such training should be "at 100 percent physical ability with zero percent stress level." Someone worried about family problems or not having enough money probably won't make it.

Details of SFQC training are not public knowledge. In general terms, the course is "individual cross country land navigation." This probably means the soldier is required to find his way through the wilderness alone. There are also swimming tests, runs along an obstacle course, and rucksack marches.

Sometimes counterterrorist groups from England, France, Germany, Israel, and Australia join Americans at Fort Bragg, and sometimes they all take advanced training in another area of the country (the Arizona desert, for instance) or in another area of the world (the Central American jungles, for example).

Delta Force Training

After the general training comes the special training for those few who are chosen to join Delta Force. The Delta Force training compound at Fort Bragg is "behind the fence" and open only to those with top clearance. It is reported to have outstanding facilities. There is an Olympic-size swimming pool, the latest kinds of gym equipment, and numerous shooting facilities.

A three-story climbing wall is used for practice. So is a section of a wide-body passenger airplane. There are mock-ups of trains and buses. One building has the nickname "House of Horrors." It is designed to teach ops how to assault a building held by terrorists.

Delta Force trainees must pass a twenty-four-day trial designed to select those who can withstand high levels of

Delta Force operatives receive training for recapturing an airliner.

physical and mental stress. The regimen includes carrying a fifty-five-pound (twenty-five-kilogram) rucksack for more than eight miles on a limited amount of food and four hours of sleep. Sometimes soldiers must march carrying sand-filled dummies, as if they were rescuing wounded comrades.

In a training exercise, Special Forces troops execute a search of a building. Delta Force members practice missions in many simulated environments so they will be prepared for every possible real-life emergency.

Delta Force trainees have to prove they are able to survive alone in isolated rugged terrain, day or night. If they have no food with them, they must find ways to get food from the land around them, even if that means eating insects and lizards. They learn to stay out of sight, to hunt stealthily, and to pinpoint their target.

They must know their weapons so well that they can clear a jammed weapon while they are running for cover. They must be able to assemble and disassemble a jeep in loose sand while under fire. They have to be able to recognize types of weapons blindfolded and load them in an instant.

Sharpshooting practice involves more than hitting a target. Trainees must practice selective firing—deciding whether or not to shoot a target. A terrorist may hold a hostage in front of him as a shield. The Delta Force sharpshooter has only seconds to make up his mind whether to fire or not.

Trainees are taught all the martial arts and practice them constantly so that if they are disarmed, they can still win in combat with karate or kickboxing. They learn to

Special Forces operatives clean and dismantle their weapons in preparation for an upcoming mission.

use knife blades skillfully and quickly, even long-blade (machete) techniques.

Mental Training

Some of the mental training comes from schoolbooks. Delta Force ops learn as much as they can about the world—its history, geography, and different cultural groups. The languages they learn allow them to slip in and out of enemy territory undercover and to understand the plans they hear by electronic eavesdropping.

They also exercise their brains in learning how to gather information and how to determine what's important and what's true. They learn about surveillance techniques and technologies and keep up with new computer software.

Psychological testing is a very important part of Delta Force training. The unit does not want cold-blooded killers or people who store up a lot of anger and then suddenly take it out on everyone around them. They don't want someone who is depressed, anxious, or insecure. The program teaches ops how to handle strong emotions, like fear and sorrow. It encourages them to build friendships and develop a sense of humor.

Special ops must be able to take hazing, which is much harsher than merely teasing. In his book, *Killing Pablo,* Mark Bowden tells the story of a Mexican-American soldier who wanted to join Delta Force. He was taunted about his ethnic background and told he wasn't "really" an American. This made him angry, but he had to control his temper because he knew it was a test. Then he was told he failed the test and would have to take the whole training program over. Even though he was very upset to hear that, he stayed calm and agreed to do it. A few minutes later he heard he had passed after all. Telling him he failed was also part of the test.

An aerial view of Fort Bragg's simulated prisoner-of-war camp. Special Forces troops receive training in interrogation techniques here. The camp is modeled on real North Vietnamese POW camps.

Delta Force ops who choose to specialize, in medicine or aviation for instance, must receive more education. But training never stops for all Delta Force ops. They have to stay in the best condition possible, mentally and physically. They must keep current on world affairs and learn the latest technology. Their brains must stay wide awake.

Warfare in the twenty-first century is likely to be "Delta-Force style"—with small groups of elite troopers who use intelligence and technology to fight terrorists or warlords, rather than all-out battles between nations. They may not even be identified as "army" or "navy" or "marine," but just as special ops who swoop into a hot spot, accomplish their mission, and leave as quickly and quietly as possible. Delta Force today is the prototype for the soldier of tomorrow.

Glossary

counterterrorism All efforts to stop terrorism, including combat, gathering information, and educating people.

intelligence Information concerning an enemy or possible enemy.

NATO The North Atlantic Treaty Organization. An international organization created in 1949 for purposes of collective security.

Night Stalkers The 160th Special Operations Aviation Regiment (SOAR), made up of high-tech helicopters.

rendezvous A prearranged meeting place.

SEALs The U.S. Navy special ops force (SEa Air Land).

smart weapons Weapons with microchips in them that direct them where to go.

SOF Special operations forces; this includes all branches of the military.

terrorism The unlawful use of force or violence with the intention of intimidating or influencing societies or governments.

For More Information

Secretary of the Army

101 Army Pentagon
Washington, DC 20310-1010
Web site: http://www.army.mil

Special Operations Command

Fort Bragg, NC 28310
(910) 396-0011
Web site: http://www.socom.mil

Web Sites

Due to the changing nature of Internet links, the Rosen Publishing Group, Inc., has developed an online list of Web sites related to the subject of this book. This site is updated regularly. Please use this link to access the list:

http://www.rosenlinks.com/iso/defo

For Further Reading

Collins, Robert F. *Basic Training: What to Expect and How to Prepare*. New York: The Rosen Publishing Group, Inc., 1988.

Collins, Robert F. *Reserve Officers Training Corps: Campus Pathways to Service Commissions*. New York: The Rosen Publishing Group, Inc., 1987.

Haney, Eric L. *Inside Delta Force: The Story of America's Elite Counterterrorist Unit*. New York: Delacorte Press, 2002.

Tomajczyk, Stephen. *U.S. Elite Counter-Terrorist Forces*. Osceola, WI: Motorbooks International, 1997.

Webster-Doyle, Terrence. *Operation Warhawk: How Young People Become Warriors*. Middlebury, VT: Education for Peace, 1993.

Weintraub, Aileen. *Life Inside the Military Academy*. New York: Children's Press, 2002.

Bibliography

Beckwith, Charlie A., and Donald Knox. *Delta Force*. San Diego, CA: Harcourt Brace Jovanovich, 1983.

Bell, Garnett "Bill." "Chargin' Charlie Beckwith at Bien Hoa." *Vietnam*. Retrieved January 2002 (http://militaryhistory.about.com/library/prm/blcharlesbeckwith1.htm?terms=beckwith).

Bowden, Mark. *Killing Pablo: The Hunt for the World's Great Outlaw*. New York: Atlantic Monthly Press, 2001.

Brown, Stuart F. "The Counterterror Arsenal." *Fortune*, October 15, 2001.

Cooperman, Alan. "Terror Strikes Again." *U.S. News & World Report*, August 17, 1998.

Hunter, Thomas B. "Operation Desert Storm: Scud Hunting on the Ground." *Special Operations Journal*, 1997. Retrieved January 2002 (http://www.specialoperations.com/Army?Delta_Force/scuds.html).

Newman, Richard J. "Hunting War Criminals." *U.S News & World Report*, July 6, 1998.

Index

About the Author

Betty Burnett, a historian, lives in St. Louis, Missouri.

Credits

Cover, pp. 1, 45, © Hans Halberstadt/Military Stock Photo; pp. 4, 48 © Leif Skoogfors/Corbis; pp. 9, 17, 33, 38, 53 © Reuters NewMedia Inc./Corbis; pp. 10, 13, 14, 23, 36, 46 © AP/Wide World Photos; pp. 19, 28 © Bettmann/Corbis; p. 41 © Corbis; p. 52 © Jeffrey L. Rotman/Corbis; p. 54 © Peter Turnley/Corbis; p. 56 © Patrick Allen,The Military Picture Library.

Editor

Christine Poolos

Design and Layout

Les Kanturek